Woman Let Go
Forgiveness Journal

Karen McCracken

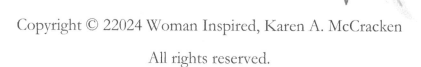

Woman Let Go

Dedication

Woman Let Go and the Woman Inspired series of books are from my heart, for God's glory. For every time I've been hurt, rejected, dismissed, and devalued, He has reminded me I am loved. Through His amazing example of grace, He has prompted me to be a forgiver of others, and of myself. All glory, credit, honor and praise to Him.

He has saved me from my iniquity, my flaws, and my desire to control that which I cannot control. No matter the mistakes I've made or wrongs I've been unable to right, He has graciously, compassionately, come alongside me, filled me with His love, and blessed me with forgiveness that I do not deserve.

By Jesus Christ's passionate example of forgiveness, I've come to embrace the truth that every Christian's quest to be Christ-like absolutely cannot be fulfilled without releasing the grip that unforgiveness has over our lives.

For those who hold on to unforgiveness, this book is for you. My hope and prayer is that within these pages you find the hope and help you need in order to let go.

♡   Karen

This Forgiveness Journal was designed to help guide you through your forgiveness journey, as outlined in the book **Woman Let Go – Release the Grip of Unforgiveness**. Within these pages are prompts taken directly from the end of each chapter in the book, as well as scripture, and plenty of space for you to take personal notes, and keep record of your progress as you grow in your knowledge of how to forgive others and yourself.

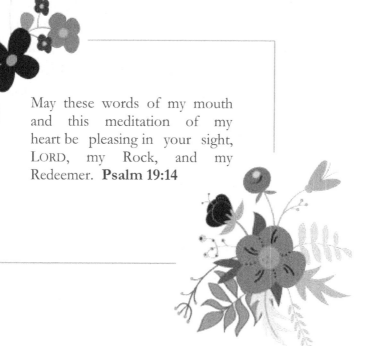

May these words of my mouth and this meditation of my heart be pleasing in your sight, LORD, my Rock, and my Redeemer. **Psalm 19:14**

Please note: If you have bad dreams, memories that haunt you, anger you can't seem to get rid of, and serious side effects from these, such as drug or alcohol use, binging, purging, self-harm, abuse, explosive anger, and thoughts of suicide or homicide, please seek professional help and assistance as you may have PTSD from your experiences. This book is not intended to take the place of any type of mental health, emotional, or ministerial counseling. Just know that in your process, God's got you, and though I may not know you, God does, and you are being prayed for.

What is forgiveness? According to Miriam Webster, forgiving means "To stop feeling anger toward someone or something; to cease to feel resentment against someone or something and to pardon." To pardon is defined as "the excusing of an offense without exacting a penalty." That's what Jesus did for us. He forgave us. He excused us, without exacting a penalty. He took the penalty for us.

Scriptural Emphasis

Matthew 6:14-15 - If you forgive those who sin against you, your heavenly Father will forgive you. But if you refuse to forgive others, your Father will not forgive your sins.

John14:15-16 - If you love me, obey my commandments. And I will ask the Father, and he will give you another advocate, who will never leave you.

Woman Let Go:
After reading the chapter, **What is forgiveness?,** take time to pray and respond to the prompts at the end of the chapter. Remember, there's no rush. This isn't a race to see who can be the most obedient, the quickest.

The path to releasing the grip of unforgiveness is a journey only you can take, one step at a time. It's personal between you and Jesus. When you take the time to pray, meditate on His Word and understand the truth of what forgiveness is, the journey even has unexpected beauty along the path.

"The most influential person in your life is the one you refuse to forgive."
Unknown

3

Woman of God, Let Go:

- Do you know if you're holding on to unforgiveness?
  Some people do. Instantly when the topic of forgiveness is
  brought up, they know who and what they haven't
  forgiven. Some of us even justify it by saying, "If God
  wanted me to forgive, He would have made a way for me
  to do that already." Well, now is your time. He's making a
  way now. If you already know of people you haven't
  forgiven then start making your list so you can go through
  the process it takes to finally forgive.

---

notes

notes

notes

Woman of God Let Go:
- Are you unsure if you're harboring unforgiveness and yet, see the signs that perhaps you are? Take the time to write down people you believe you have forgiven and pray over each one to make sure you're not harboring unforgiveness. Take it to the Lord in prayer. As you do, in quiet prayerful time, go over each one and analyze it through the lens of the "3 signs you're holding on to unforgiveness" I shared in this chapter. Take notes if needed. Let God show you if and where you're harboring unforgiveness so you can work through the process of forgiving.

_____

_____

_____

_____

_____

_____

_____

_____

_____

notes

notes

notes

notes

Woman of God Let Go:

- Consider the truth in this quote: "The most influential person in your life is the one you refuse to forgive." If there's someone who's taking up more time, space, thought, and emotion in your life than Jesus, then pray for the Holy Spirit to show you why. Seek the Lord for release from the unforgiveness that has undue influence over your daily life. Take note of whom and what negative thoughts or unforgiveness is influencing you the

_____

_____

_____

_____

_____

_____

_____

_____

_____

_____

_____

_____

notes

notes

_____

_____

_____

_____

_____

_____

_____

_____

_____

_____

_____

_____

_____

_____

_____

_____

_____

_____

_____

_____

notes

notes

What did Jesus say about forgiveness? Several places in the Bible reference forgiveness. For this chapter, we're going to get to the crux of what Jesus said about forgiveness through what are likely the most quoted Bible verses on the subject. ~ **"Then Peter came to him and asked, "Lord, how often should I forgive someone who sins against me? Seven times?", "No, not seven times," Jesus replied, "but seventy times seven!"** Matthew 18:21-22 ~

Scriptural Emphasis

Matthew 18:21-22
"Then Peter came to him and asked, "Lord, how often should I forgive someone who sins against me? Seven times?", "No, not seven times," Jesus replied, "but seventy times seven!"

Read also: **Luke 6:37, 1 John 1:9**, and **Mark 11:25**

Woman Let Go:
After reading the chapter, **What does Jesus say about forgiveness?**, take time to pray and respond to the prompts at the end of the chapter. Refer back to the chapters as you go through each section, responding prayerfully. Take the time to reflect on what you've learned in this chapter about what Jesus said about forgiveness. Reflect, pray, meditate on His Word, and understand the truth of what forgiveness truly is versus what the world tells us it is. Write down your thoughts and feelings.

The definition of pardon is "to excuse or forgive without exacting punishment." That's what Jesus did for us. He took the punishment for us." - K. McCracken

Woman of God Let Go:

- Take time to read and pray over **Matthew 18:21-22**. Ask the Lord to shine the light on where you've forgiven and then taken it back. Keep notes so you can work through the process of forgiving once and for all. As you know you've forgiven, take a marker and black out that transgression, looking at it no more. No longer keep a record of it on paper or in the back of your mind. Let the Lord show you how to release the grip that unforgiveness has had on you.

_____

_____

_____

_____

_____

_____

_____

_____

_____

_____

_____

notes

notes

notes

notes

Woman of God Let Go:

- In your Forgiveness Journal and on some index cards, slips of paper, write down, "It is finished: Keepin' in 490". Put them in your Bible, in your purse, on your bathroom mirror, on the dash of your car, on your fridge, and anyplace else you'll see them on a regular basis. When you're having a day where past transgressions from others or yourself come creeping back at you, the reminders will be there to Keep it 490. Resist the temptation to pick that forgiveness up and turn it back into unforgiveness. God does not ask us to do that which we are incapable of doing. While it takes effort, it's totally possible. We usually need His help doing it and most likely you will need practice, but it IS possible to forgive and say "It is finished". Make a list of places you want to put your reminders as well as additional Bible verses that might help remind you to continue to let go of unforgiveness.

---

notes

notes

notes

Forget about the forgetting. Forgiving then forgetting isn't just impossible, it's also dangerous. We need to remember the lessons that come with the process of forgiving and the realities of what has happened in our lives. Jesus is the one who said that He would cast our sins as far as the East is from the West, remembering them no more. The Bible says we are to forgive others but it doesn't say forget

Scriptural Emphasis

Hebrew 8:12
And I will forgive their wickedness, and I will never again remember their sins.

Joshua 1:9
Have I not commanded you? Be strong and courageous. Do not be afraid; do not be discouraged, for the LORD your God will be with you wherever you go.

Woman Let Go:
After reading the chapter, **Forget about the forgetting,** take time to pray and respond to the prompts at the end of the chapter. There are places for you to write down your thoughts on the following pages. Have you been pretending you can forget then been unable to forgive?. If so, you're not alone. Take the time to seek the Lord's guidance and ask Him to shine a light on the truth of what you have believed and what you still need to forgive in others and yourself.

"Forgiving is Christ-like. We were made to be able to forgive and commanded to do so."
K. McCracken

28

Woman of God Let Go:

- If you have engrained in your mind that you must "forgive and forget" then I encourage you to read these scriptures that talk about the Lord's grace and mercy. See for yourself what true grace looks like.
    - Psalm 103:10-13
    - Matthew 18:23-35
    - Luke 7:41-50
    - Matthew 18:21-35
- Write down how these scriptures affect you, if at all. Consider what Jesus' grace has looked like in your life.

_____

_____

_____

_____

_____

_____

_____

_____

_____

_____

_____

notes

notes

notes

Woman of God Let Go:

- Do you have things you've forgiven others for and yet they keep coming up at you? Do you have consistent reminders of those events? Have you truly forgiven or did you merely attempt to forget the pain, hoping that in forgetting, the forgiving would also be done? Take the time to talk about those things with the Lord. Ask Him to shine a light on your heart and mind so you can identify if you've actually forgiven them or if you've just pretended to forget, hoping that effort alone would be enough. Write down those things that you've held the tightest to and pray for the Lord to help you work through them.

_____

_____

_____

_____

_____

_____

_____

notes

notes

notes

notes

Woman of God Let Go:

- Are you caught in a cycle of saying you forgave, trying to forget, and then allowing the same thing to happen over and over again? Are you stuck in a pattern of letting someone hurt you and are unsure of how to get off that roller coaster? Repeat to yourself daily that forgetting is not the same as forgiving. Write down the scriptures in the Bible about what forgiveness and grace are and work to memorize them or keep them handy. When you're tempted to just push a memory out of your head of someone you haven't forgiven, take it straight to the Lord and remind yourself that your goal is to forgive and be obedient in doing so. Write notes here to encourage yourself to continue to work on forgiving those you have not yet forgiven.

_____

_____

_____

_____

_____

_____

_____

notes

notes

notes

notes

Forgiveness is healthier than forgiveness – God knew what the National Library of Medicine's PubMed webpage only recently found out. It cites a medical research paper from February 2022 as follows: "Empirical studies have shown that forgiveness decreases anger, anxiety, and depression and increases self-esteem and hopefulness for the future." And when we talk about health we can't ignore the most important health, which is spiritual. Spiritual health affects us mentally and physically. Holding on to unforgiveness can affect your life in many ways, including your mental and physical health.

Scriptural Emphasis

Ephesians 4:32
Be kind and compassionate to one another, forgiving each other, just as in Christ God forgave you.

Read also:
Matthew 7:24-27
John 15:10-14

Woman Let Go:
After reading the chapter, **Forgiveness is healthier than unforgiveness**, take time to pray before responding to the prompts at the end of the chapter.
Consider your own mental and physical health. Keep track of your spiritual, emotional, and mental health. Consider seeking a professional for help as God leads if you're holding on to unforgiveness that is affecting your health.

"When we tend to the needs of our soul by being diligent in our prayer life, worship, Bible study, meditation, and our quest to be obedient to what the Word says and what God leads us to do in our lifetime, we're setting ourselves up to feel better inside and out." - K . McCracken

Woman of God Let Go:

- Have you observed unforgiveness affecting your health in any way? Take some time to think and pray about it. Make a list of ways that unforgiveness may have affected your mental, emotional, spiritual, and physical health.

_____

_____

_____

_____

_____

_____

_____

_____

_____

_____

_____

_____

notes

notes

notes

Woman of God Let Go:

- Is there a particular thing, action, or person you have not forgiven that is affecting your health? Are you stuffing your emotions deep down, pretending to forgive and forget and then allowing it to affect your health? Document it. This is something you'll want to address so you can become fully obedient to Jesus' call to forgive, AND become healthier.

_____

_____

_____

_____

_____

_____

_____

_____

_____

_____

_____

notes

notes

notes

Forgiving Self - Unless we acknowledge that we've sinned and taken responsibility for it in some form or fashion, we won't understand the depth to which our actions have affected our mindset, and decisions. Without repenting of our sins, we can't fully embrace the reasons we need forgiveness from Jesus or from ourselves. Once we embrace this truth, and realize that He has forgiven, it becomes easier to forgive ourselves.

Scriptural Emphasis

Romans 8:1-2
So now there is no condemnation for those who belong to Christ Jesus. And because you belong to him, the power of the life-giving Spirit has freed you from the power of sin that leads to death."

1 John 1:9
If we confess our sins, he is faithful and just and will forgive us our sins and purify us from all unrighteousness.

Woman Let Go:
After reading the chapter, **Forgiving Self,** take time to pray and respond to the prompts at the end of the chapter. Don't forget to read and consider the 3 signs that you may still be holding on to unforgiveness towards yourself.

Take time to pray and let the Lord show you things you may not be aware of that you've been holding on to or holding against yourself. If you realize you haven't truly repented and taken those things to the Lord, then do so…and then work to embrace the truth that He wants you to also forgive yourself.

"I will confess my rebellion to the LORD." And you forgave me! All my guilt is gone."
Psalm 32:5

Woman of God Let Go:

- Do you have a list in your head of things you're holding against yourself? Sins and wrong-doings you think are unforgivable? They are not unforgivable. Go to the Lord with that list. Old sins, new sins, all sins. Take them to the Lord and ask Him to shine the light on them so you can deal with them. Seek His forgiveness and strength to repent.

---

notes

notes

notes

notes

notes

Woman of God Let Go:

- To make amends or not make amends? When it comes to making amends we have to be cautious. Often our desire to make amends with someone comes out of a desire to rid ourselves of guilt. The rule of thumb here is the same as the rule of thumb for people going through a 12-step recovery program. Lesson 16 in the Celebrate Recovery step program is about making Amends. Their rule of thumb is: "Evaluate all my relationships. Offer forgiveness to those who have hurt me and make amends for harm I've done to others, <u>except when to do so would harm them or others</u>"

  If your goal in making amends, apologizing, or offering some sort of restitution is to ease your own guilt, don't do it. Let Jesus guide you. Be open to the Holy Spirit's prompting in this and be without doubt before you proceed. If reaching out to someone will cause harm and undue stress to them or someone they love, then it's not the course of action you should take. If that's the case then let it go and focus on simply being obedient to God rather than attempting to make amends.

  If you feel led to make amends, journal here about who, and the possibilities of where and when. Be cautious, be purposeful, and let the Lord guide you with the right words and wisdom.

notes

notes

notes

notes

Woman of God Let Go:

- Offering forgiveness to others, confessing your sins, and seeking forgiveness from God is the first step in the process of stopping your own guilt and self-punishment. When you're able to do these things, it frees you to forgive yourself as well. To become free from the grip of unforgiveness though, we have to remember that pouring out those transgressions to God and embracing the freedom that comes from repentance is necessary for you to release that grip of unforgiveness you hold over yourself. Now is the time to let go and start your journey to release the grip that unforgiveness of yourself may hold on you. Keep track here of what you're praying to let go of, and the praises for what you have let go of..

_____

_____

_____

_____

_____

_____

_____

_____

notes

notes

notes

notes

notes

notes

notes

The cycle of unforgiveness – If you know you're caught in a bad cycle, hold on to faith. Through Biblical perspectives, scripture, and prayer, remember that others have gone before you and been able to let go of unforgiveness. If others were able to finally let go, believe that you can too. Don't give up. Take heart because even though holding on to unforgiveness, and the side effects of it may seem like an endless cycle, with the Lord's help everyone has the ability to put an end to it.

Scriptural Emphasis

James 1:5
If any of you lacks wisdom, let him ask God, who gives generously to all without reproach, and it will be given him.

Read also:

John 14:15-16
Psalm 1:1-2

Woman Let Go:
After reading **The cycle of unforgiveness** chapter, take time to pray for the Lord to help you identify areas of your life where you're stuck in a cycle. Seek answers and discernment for where perhaps you've ended up holding on to unforgiveness, and it has then created a pattern of resentment and thoughts of retaliation. Ask for forgiveness and then listen to what He tells you.

"Without forgiveness, a human's life is governed by an endless cycle of resentment and retaliation."
Robert Assagioli

Woman of God Let Go:

- Go now before the throne of God and seek Him to show you through His eyes if you have any past or present unforgiveness gripping you. Write down what He shows you as you pray for guidance.

_____

_____

_____

_____

_____

_____

_____

_____

_____

_____

_____

_____

_____

notes

notes

notes

Woman of God Let Go:

- Write down the insights, situations, events, and people God places on your heart as you pray for Him to show you where you haven't truly forgiven and where unforgiveness still has a grip on you.

_____

_____

_____

_____

_____

_____

_____

_____

_____

_____

_____

_____

notes

notes

notes

Woman of God Let Go:

- Now pray for God to illuminate any chain reaction that has happened in your life because of your unforgiveness. Are there bad choices you've made, relationships you've severed, people you've lashed out at, or purposefully hurt because you ended up in a cycle of resentment and retaliation? Write these down and ask Him to strengthen you through this process. Keep this so you can come back to this list again in later but continue to pray in your quiet time for His revelation in this process.

_____

_____

_____

_____

_____

_____

_____

_____

_____

notes

notes

notes

notes

A daily attitude of forgiveness - Unforgiveness, no matter who is harboring it, festers. It becomes an infected injury in our minds and our emotions. It eventually causes us to become spiritually stagnant. Making a practice of forgiving often and without bias is essential to healthy Christian living and healthy relationships but it's also essential for healthy spiritual growth in our walk with the Lord.

Scriptural Emphasis

Philippians 4:12-13 - I know what it is to be in need, and I know what it is to have plenty. I have learned the secret of being content in any and every situation, whether well-fed or hungry, whether living in plenty or in want. I can do all this through him who gives me strength.

Read also:
1 Peter 4:10-11

Woman Let Go:
After reading the chapter, **A daily attitude of forgiveness**, pray and talk to the Lord about where your heart and mind is concerning daily forgiveness. Do you allow yourself to sit in the hurt past mistakes? If so, is it affecting your current daily ability to forgive with ease and with a Christ-like determination? How difficult is it for you to see that God is bigger than all that? He is bigger than all your stress, past mistakes, hurts and worries. Pray and meditate on building up your attitude of daily forgiveness.

"In the blink of an eye, everything can change. So forgive often and love with all your heart. You may never have the chance again."
Zig Ziglar

Woman of God Let Go:

- Are there every day hurts, offenses, or misunderstandings you've not forgiven? Are they building, one on top of another and creating a wall between you and someone else in your life? Take time to analyze your closest relationships first. If you're harboring anything against someone else for a minor offense, take it to the Lord. Determine within yourself, committing to the Lord that you will forgive and let go of this kind of unforgiveness on a daily basis before it festers. Write down what He shows you about your attitude of daily forgiveness.

_____

_____

_____

_____

_____

_____

_____

_____

_____

notes

notes

notes

Woman of God Let Go:

- It may take practice, but on a daily basis start to release offenses soon after they happen. Aggravation, insults, feeling slighted and ignored, teased, or demeaned are all things that happen regularly in today's culture. Be determined to speak out to the Lord. Vent to Him, rather than getting into an argument with someone else. Ask Him to help you do so. Call out the offense and proclaim that you forgive that person/people. Forgiving breaks any power that offense and hurt have over you, and takes far less time out of your day than holding on to hurt and anger. Try writing out what you forgive and praying for the person you're forgiving. Perhaps he or she is in need of being uplifted, whether they realize it or not.

_____

_____

_____

_____

_____

_____

notes

notes

notes

notes

notes

notes

notes

notes

Forgiving like Jesus - For any Christian, the daily quest to be Christ-like is ever-present. That doesn't mean we can reach the status of perfection Jesus has. It means we are to be 'like' Christ...as much like Him as we possibly can. That cannot exclude the whole action of forgiving others merely because so many people think it's nearly impossible to do.

Scriptural Emphasis

Ephesians 4:31-32
Get rid of all bitterness, rage and anger, brawling and slander, along with every form of malice. Be kind and compassionate to one another, forgiving each other, just as in Christ God forgave you.
Read also:
1 John 1:9
Matthew 6:14-15

Woman Let Go:
After reading the chapter, **Forgiving like Jesus,** take time to pray and respond to the prompts at the end of the chapter. Remember, when you feel as if you've failed at letting go of unforgiveness or it takes you longer to forgive than you know it should, take solace in the words of Billy Graham. "Being a Christian is more than just an instantaneous conversion - it is a daily process whereby you grow to be more and more like Christ."

"To be Christian means to forgive the inexcusable because God has forgiven the inexcusable in you".
C.S. Lewis

Woman of God Let Go:

- I encourage you to intentionally muster up the effort it takes to forgive like Jesus; with grace and compassion. Yes, it takes work but the peace that comes from being able to lay your head down at night and truly rest is well worth it. More than that, the peace that comes from honoring God and what He told you to do in forgiving others and yourself is a kind of peace that lasts.

     1. Go through your previous chapter notes and choose some people/things you need to forgive. Don't take them on all at once. Just choose 2 or 3.

     2. Go through the steps in this chapter for each thing you need to forgive. Pray and ask the Lord to show you what scriptures to write down and guide you to the quotes that will suit you best as you start this quest to systematically do the work you need to do in order to take your thoughts captive and release them from the grip of unforgiveness. Each time your mind goes off on a path of anger and obsessive thoughts about each of these you need to forgive, use the scripture and quotes you chose to help redirect your thoughts, and control which emotions you choose to feel.

notes

notes

notes

notes

notes

notes

notes

notes

notes

notes

Woman of God Let Go:

- Looking at **2 Corinthians 10: 3-5** it says, **"For though we live in the world, we do not wage war as the world does. The weapons we fight with are not the weapons of the world. On the contrary, they have divine power to demolish strongholds. We demolish arguments and every pretense that sets itself up against the knowledge of God, and we take captive every thought to make it obedient to Christ."** Pray this out loud in your prayer time as often as you need to remind yourself that it is possible to take your thoughts captive and in doing so, you honor God.

---

notes

notes

notes

notes

notes

notes

Woman of God Let Go:

- Remember, unforgiveness only has power over you as you let it. You can release the grip it has on your life and not make forgiving someone or something a one-time thing. Forgiveness should be a constant mindset that draws you closer and closer to being Christ-like. There is no other action, deed, thought, or way of life more Christ-like than that of living a life of perpetual forgiveness and tenderheartedness towards others.

- Serve! Find a place to serve; a place to turn your pain into purpose. Remember, there is no greater path to getting out of your own way than to get in the path of purpose. Start making calls and contacts this week, finding a place to put your time and energy.

- Write down your thoughts, feelings, fears and excitement about the possibility of putting yourself on a path to purpose. Jot down some ideas of where you want to inquire about sharing your talents and your time.

_____

_____

_____

_____

_____

_____

notes

notes

notes

notes

notes

notes

Amazing stories of forgiveness – Forgiving others and then sharing the experience as a testimony is not bragging about whom you are or what you've done but is an act of glorifying God. Without the strength and love that comes from the advocate – the Holy Spirit – and the truth in God's Word, forgiveness wouldn't be possible. Don't forget that forgiving others is the most Christ-like thing you can do.

Scriptural Emphasis

Colossians 3:12
Therefore, as God's chosen people, holy and dearly loved, clothe yourselves with compassion, kindness, humbleness, gentleness and patience.

Psalm 105:1
Give thanks to the LORD and proclaim his greatness. Let the whole world know what he has done.
Read also:
Ephesians 4:2-3

Woman Let Go:
After reading the chapter, **Amazing stories of forgiveness,** consider the true stories and what you can learn from them. Are their things you don't believe you could embrace or know you should do but don't feel you have the strength to do? Take it to Jesus. Seek His help for the guidance and courage you need to be obedient.

"For God so loved the world that he gave his one and only Son, that <u>who so ever</u> believes in him shall not perish but have eternal life."
John 3:16

Woman of God Let Go:

- I encourage you to read the verses in **Luke 23: 26-49** and remember or perhaps learn for the first time, how Jesus died all in the name of forgiveness. That forgiveness is for all who come to Him, repent and accept it. He is our example, our strength, our Rock, and our Redeemer. Allow Him to be.

- If you haven't released the grip of unforgiveness, perhaps you're in a position similar to where I was in needing to immerse yourself in the truth of grace and humbleness. Find scripture that points you to true grace and humbleness as shown in God's Word. Write it down, pray over it, and ask God to change your heart to one that embraces grace and start your forgiveness journey over with a humble heart.

_____

_____

_____

_____

_____

_____

_____

notes

notes

notes

notes

Woman of God Let Go:

- Are you walking around with scales on your eyes? Blinders? Are you unable to see how God is moving or what He's doing in your life or perhaps in the life of someone you've refused to forgive? Pray and ask Him to remove your blinders, giving you greater discernment and the ability to see people through His eyes, rather than your own.

- Do you have a story of forgiveness to tell? Write it down, or record it. Share it with others. I believe Jesus is calling us to share with others our stories of forgiveness. Let your forgiveness of others and yourself be a part of your testimony, for there is no greater witness to living a Christ-like life than to do as Christ did and forgive. Living in a world that tells us to forgive and forget or to seek revenge and get even, we're sorely lacking in the true stories of successful forgiveness. In sharing your story, simple or complex, deeply personal or painful, consistent or exhausting, you may help someone else who is struggling to forgive.

_____

_____

_____

_____

_____

notes

notes

notes

notes

notes

notes

ADDITIONAL SCRIPTURE, QUOTES AND ENCOURAGEMENT

May these words of my mouth and this meditation of my heart be pleasing in your sight, LORD, my Rock, and my Redeemer. **Psalm 19:14**

And without faith, it is impossible to please God, because anyone who comes to him must believe that he exists and that he rewards those who earnestly seek him. **Hebrews 11:6**

Do not conform to the pattern of this world, but be transformed by the renewing of your mind. Then you will be able to test and approve what God's will is - his good, pleasing, and perfect will. **Romans 12:2**

Be kind and compassionate to one another, forgiving each other, just as in Christ God forgave you. **Ephesians 4:32**

If we confess our sins, he is faithful and just and will forgive us our sins and purify us from all unrighteousness. **1 John 1:9**

For if you forgive other people when they sin against you, your heavenly Father will also forgive you. But if you do not forgive others their sins, your Father will not forgive your sins. **Matthew 6:14-15**

On justice and judgment

Consequently, just as one trespass resulted in condemnation for all people, so also one righteous act resulted in justification and life for all people. For just as through the disobedience of the one man the many were made sinners, so also through the obedience of the one man, the many will be made righteous. **Romans 5:18-19**

Love and faithfulness meet together; righteousness and peace kiss each other. Faithfulness springs forth from the earth, and righteousness looks down from heaven. **Psalm 85:10-11**

Righteousness and justice are the foundation of your throne; love and faithfulness go before you. **Psalm 89:14**

God "will repay each person according to what they have done." To those who by persistence in doing good seek glory, honor, and immortality, he will give eternal life. But for those who are self-seeking and who reject the truth and follow evil, there will be wrath and anger. There will be trouble and distress for every human being who does evil: first for the Jew, then for the Gentile; but glory, honor, and peace for everyone who does good: first for the Jew, then for the Gentile. For God does not show favoritism. **Romans 2:6-11**

About obedience

"Therefore everyone who hears these words of mine and puts them into practice is like a wise man who built his house on the rock. The rain came down, the streams rose, and the winds blew and beat against that house; yet it did not fall, because it had its foundation on the rock. But everyone who hears these words of mine and does not put them into practice is like a foolish man who built his house on sand. The rain came down, the streams rose, and the winds blew and beat against that house, and it fell with a great crash." **Matthew 7:24-27**

If you keep my commands, you will remain in my love, just as I have kept my Father's commands and remain in his love. I have told you this so that my joy may be in you and that your joy may be complete. My command is this: Love each other as I have loved you. Greater love has no one than this: to lay down one's life for one's friends. You are my friends if you do what I command. **John 15:10-14**

Blessed is the one who does not walk in step with the wicked or stand in the way that sinners take or sit in the company of mockers, but whose delight is in the law of the LORD, and who meditates on his law day and night. **Psalm 1:1-2**

Do not merely listen to the word, and so deceive yourselves. Do what it says. Anyone who listens to the word but does not do what it says is like someone who looks at his face in a mirror and, after looking at himself, goes away and immediately forgets what he looks like. But whoever looks intently into the perfect law that gives freedom, and continues in it—not forgetting what they have heard, but doing it, they will be blessed in what they do. **James 1:22-25**

Encouraging quotes

The goodness you receive from God is a treasure to share with others. – Elizabeth George

Don't judge other people more harshly than you want God to judge you. – Marie T. Freeman

When you are weary and everything seems to be going wrong, you can still utter these four words: "I trust You, Jesus." – Sarah Young

The steady discipline of intimate friendship with Jesus results in men becoming like Him. – Harry Emerson Fosdick

God is interested in developing your character. At times He lets you proceed, but He will never let you go too far without discipline to bring you back. In your relationship with God, He may let you make a wrong decision. Then the Spirit of God causes you to recognize that it is not God's will. He guides you back to the right path. – Henry Blackaby

It hurts when God has to PRY things out of our hands! – Corrie Ten Boom

"Forgiveness is a powerful expression of the love within our soul." - Anthony Douglas

"Forgiveness is above all a personal choice, a decision of the heart to go against the natural instinct to pay back evil with evil." - Pope John Paul II

"To forgive is to set a prisoner free and discover that the prisoner was you."- Lewis Smedes

"In the shadow of my hurt, forgiveness feels like a decision to reward my enemy. But in the shadow of the cross, forgiveness is merely a gift from one undeserving soul to another."-Andy Stanley

Throughout my journey to become more Christ-like in my thoughts and actions, I have learned that the most Christ-like thing I could ever do would be to forgive others. - Karen McCracken

additional notes

additional notes

additional notes

additional notes

additional notes

additional notes

additional notes

additional notes

ABOUT THE AUTHOR

Karen McCracken is the author of several books, including her 2023 Amazon Best-Selling book, Woman Stand Firm. She is also a Christian speaker and comedian who has spoken at over 350 women's conferences and retreats across the United States.

Karen hosts The Woman Inspired Podcast and was nominated for 3 Spark Media Podcasting awards. Her passion is to reach women inside and outside the church setting with the gospel message and to come alongside women in the Body of Christ with the message of hope and truth for those who feel lonely, afraid, and are drowning in an ever-changing, frightening world.

Karen is a wife, mom, avid gardener, and loves the outdoors. She's handy in the kitchen, loves to dance while she does housework, and enjoys making other people laugh.

To tune in to Karen's podcast, go to womaninspired.com or look for The Woman Inspired Podcast on your favorite podcast platform.

Made in the USA
Las Vegas, NV
14 January 2025

16354868R00089